RAPID STUDY SKILLS FOR STUDENTS: SUCCESSFUL ESSAY PLANNING POCKETBOOK

www.How2Become.com

As part of this product you have also received FREE access to online tests! To gain access, simply go to:

www.MyEducationalTests.co.uk

Get more products for passing any test at:

www.How2Become.com

Disclaimer

Every effort has been made to ensure that the information contained within this guide is accurate at the time of publication. How2Become Ltd is not responsible for anyone failing any part of any selection process as a result of the information contained within this guide. How2Become Ltd and their authors cannot accept any responsibility for any errors or omissions within this guide, however caused. No responsibility for loss or damage occasioned by any person acting, or refraining from action, as a result of the material in this publication can be accepted by How2Become Ltd.

The information within this guide does not represent the views of any third-party service or organisation

Contents

INTRODUCTION

WHY READ THIS BOOK?

As you know all too well, essays are an extremely important part of any academic career. Whether it's in the form of coursework or timed assessments in class, you'll have written many an extended written task for marks. Or, perhaps you are at the start of an academic career, and have not yet been fully acquainted with all the joys of this particular endeavour.

Either way, *Successful Essay Planning* will provide all the information and guidance you need. No matter how experienced an essay writer you are, the clear and actionable advice on every stage of the assignment-writing process is here to take your essay game to the next level.

Also, depending on what you're after, you may not need to read this book cover to cover — simply have a look at the contents section and locate the relevant content.

In any case, let's get started with the first section of the guide — note taking.

NOTE TAKING

Before starting a written project, it's highly likely that you'll need to take notes of some description. Whether it's part of your academic research, or thinking of some plot points and character arcs for creative writing, effective note taking should be high on your list of priorities. This is a deceptively difficult task – it's easy to write notes that may not be doing a lot for you. Let's look at some techniques you can employ to maximise the quality of your notes, while minimising the amount of time spent on them.

1. Keep your notes simple.

- Try to boil down your thoughts into key words and phrases;

- This will make your notes easier to revise and remember;

- Shorter, more focused notes, will help you to structure your ideas.

2. Know what you want to say.

- Although note taking could help you decide on the direction of your essay or other piece of work, it's best to go into it with clear objectives. Know what you're aiming to get out of your notes, and be selective with what you actually highlight/jot down. If it's not going to help with your specific task — don't waste time noting it down!

3. Develop your notes.

- Over time, you'll want your notes to gradually become more advanced — up until the point when you'll transform them into a detailed plan;

- Spider diagrams are a good place to start. These are useful for collecting your ideas all on one page. You can also show connections between points with drawn lines and colours;

- Then, you can flesh out these points into linear notes. Here you can organise your notes using headings and sub-headings, and underline what's most important;

- Following this stage, you'll have the basis of a detailed plan – the natural next step!

DON'T FORGET TO MIND THE GAP

Sadly, this doesn't involve an exciting trip to London; it's a simple acronym you can use to keep your note taking focused. It's particularly relevant for creative writing, and should serve to guide any research you're carrying out in preparation for embarking on your project.

Genre – When taking notes before your project, know the conventions of the genre you are aiming to write within. For example, if you are writing a horror novel, you might read and make notes from a number of horror works to ascertain what makes them fit the bill. Is it the use of characters, setting, or plot? There won't be one clear answer, but focused note taking in this way will help you to no end when writing.

Audience – Again, it is important to be mindful of who you expect to get the most out of your writing. For example, if you are aiming to write a novel that resonates with people in their twenties, you'll want to research and take notes on novels which have successfully done this. How have the writers tailored their work to their specific audience? Perhaps there is no cut-and-dry answer, but you might be surprised at the similarities between writing aimed at the same demographics.

Purpose – Similarly, during your research stages, you need to have a clear view of what you're hoping to achieve with your work. Again, this is how you will be able to carry out productive and relevant note taking. Once you know this, you can examine works which have achieved the same or similar effects. Thorough analysis like this will pay off – knowledge of *how* great writers do what they do will show in your work.

ESSAY PLANNING

The key to high grades in any assignment is planning. If you can nail a good plan and stick to it with all of your coursework, you can make sure that you cover all bases and increase your likelihood of excellence.

We have provided a flowchart designed to take you through the step-by-step process of completing an assignment – from the earliest stage of choosing a topic to submitting it and receiving feedback. You might find that some of the steps do not apply to the type of assessment that you're working on. In that case, skip the step and move onto the next one.

Let's take a quick look at each of these steps:

Choose a Topic

This will only apply to you if you've been given a choice of topics to write your assignment about. Essay-based subjects usually have a list of different questions that you can choose from, but this may differ between universities, departments, and modules. If you aren't sure, check the department website, or ask your lecturer or seminar leader.

Other subjects may be more limited in the range of topics you can write your assignment on. If this is the case, you can ignore this step.

Choose and Dissect Exact Question

Once you've chosen a topic, or been given one, you might be given a choice of the exact question. It might be tempting to jump at the question on the topic you most enjoy, but be cautious of the questions themselves. While they might cover the topic that you think you understand really well, they might approach it from an angle that you aren't comfortable with. Carefully examine each question available to you before choosing one.

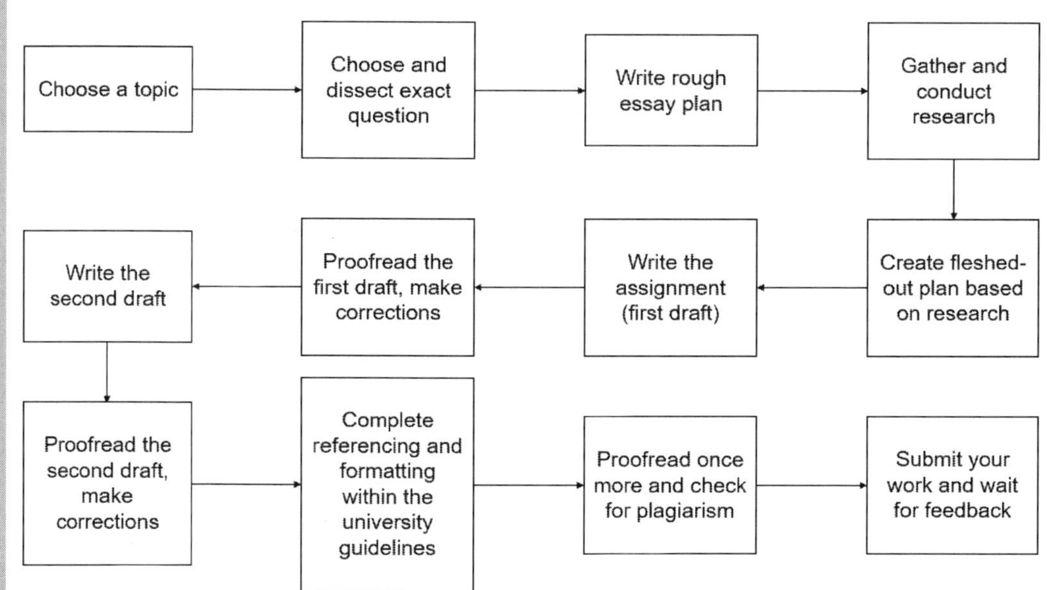

Choose a topic
Choose and dissect exact question
Write rough essay plan
Gather and conduct research
Write the second draft
Proofread the first draft, make corrections
Write the assignment (first draft)
Create fleshed-out plan based on research
Proofread the second draft, make corrections
Complete referencing and formatting within the university guidelines
Proofread once more and check for plagiarism
Submit your work and wait for feedback

After you've finished choosing a question, you need to take it apart and figure out what it's really asking of you. Keep an eye out for scope, both in terms of the scale of the area itself and how deep it expects you to go.

Write Rough Essay Plan

Once you've chosen your question and know what it's asking of you, it's time to start writing a rough plan. This won't be the final plan that you follow for the entire project – just a loose one to help you gather your thoughts for the research stage.

If you're writing an essay, try to construct a paragraph-by-paragraph plan in this stage. At the very least, you should have a good idea of what the sections of the essay or project are, and how they link together. Once you've finished doing this, you're ready to start the research phase of the essay-writing process!

Gather and Conduct Research

In this stage, you'll spend most of your time reading, working with others, or doing practical work so that you have something to support your assignment with. The exact nature of the research will depend on the subject and module that your assignment is in.

Create a Fleshed-Out Plan Based on Research

Once you've got all of your research together, you now need to apply it to your plan. If you're writing an essay, you want to look for anywhere in your plan where you've made some kind of claim. Add relevant evidence from your sources here, so that everything you're going to write in your essay is supported.

If you're doing some other kind of assignment, such as a write-up based on lab work, your entire piece will centre around your research. Again, include evidence from your own research to your plan where relevant, so your argument is well-supported.

To make things easier, try to make a note of all the page numbers and locations of everything you're citing in your work. This will save you from having to trawl through all your sources looking for the exact line and page where you got your evidence from.

Write the Assignment (First Draft)

Now that you've got a full and fleshed-out plan, it's time to write the first draft. If you've taken your planning seriously, you shouldn't need to refer to any of your sources here – just follow each point of your plan, turning the bullet points and other short notes into full sentences.

If you've already made a full plan, this stage shouldn't take long at all. The key is to follow your plan as much as possible, and turn a series of notes into a coherent, eloquent piece of writing.

Proofread the First Draft
With a first draft finished, you should now read through it at least once. At this stage, keep an eye out for spelling, grammar, and punctuation errors – you don't want your work to contain any amateur mistakes.

Here, you can also get an idea of how your work flows from point to point. If you think some bits don't work properly, or something doesn't fit, make a note of it and then you can find a solution when you write the second draft.

Write the Second Draft
Writing the second draft is less a case of re-writing your whole assignment, and more of looking at the entire piece critically and trying to re-write parts so that they're even more concise. You might feel as though this is unnecessary, but going through and rewording things can help with clarity.

Proofread the Second Draft
As with the first draft, it's important to re-read your work to make sure there are no glaring errors.

Complete Referencing and Formatting

Hopefully, you've been referencing as you go along. If so, there should be little to do in this section when it comes to referencing. Just make sure that you've followed the referencing system that your university and department have specified, such as the Harvard Referencing System. You will probably also need to write a bibliography – do this at this stage.

In addition, you should make sure that the formatting of your work meets the specifications of the department. If your work is word-processed, they might specifically request certain fonts, font sizes, and line spacing. Check the guidelines set by your department since some universities will dock points from assignments that aren't formatted correctly.

Proofread and Check for Plagiarism

In this final stage, you want to proofread your work and specifically check for plagiarism. We'll discuss plagiarism in more detail later in this chapter, but for now ensure that whenever you've used supporting evidence from a source, you've cited them properly. The aim of this is to make sure that you aren't passing off someone else's work as your own.

One way to check for plagiarism is to copy and paste sections of your own writing into a search engine. If this leads to results of places where you might have gathered ideas from, then you need to cite it as a source or remove the suspicious piece of text from your work. If you do remove it, make sure to replace it with your own work.

Universities take plagiarism very seriously, so it's important that you take extra care when checking for it.

Submit Work and Wait for Feedback

Once you get to this stage, you're basically finished. However, you still need to submit your work. Different universities, departments, and even modules might specify how to hand in your work once it's finished. Some might request a printed copy, whilst others will use an automated system where you can upload your work too. In some cases, they might request both. Your department should make their requirements clear either on their website, or in the introductory documents for the course or module.

Once your work has been submitted, you'll need to wait for it to be marked. Hopefully this won't take too long, but different universities have different standards when it comes to turnaround on assessed work.

When your work and marks are returned to you, spend some time re-reading your assignment to see where you picked up marks, and where you lost them. Hopefully, the examiner has offered some feedback alongside the marked piece of work. Make sure that you read this feedback carefully and take it on board for your next assignment. If you don't get any feedback on your work, or have any questions, get in touch with your seminar leader or lecturer.

ESSAY WRITING

Now that we've covered more general writing tips about sentences, paragraphs, and style, let's focus on the practicalities of what it's all about as a student: essay writing. Whether you are at school or university, you'll have to spend a lot of time planning, writing, and proofreading assessed work. If this sounds like a nightmare to you, then here's ten top tips on getting an amazing mark on your next essay!

1. Read the question carefully and make sure that you understand it.

There's only one thing worse than realising you've misunderstood a question halfway through writing your essay, and that's realising you've misunderstood it *after* you get your marks back. Some people like to jump into an essay as soon as they've found a question that they think is interesting. However, by being too eager, students can end up either making more work for themselves when they have to re-write their entire essay, or lose marks because they didn't fully understand the question.

Having a strong understanding of your essay title will help you to write the best answer possible. Pay attention to the scope of the question, and look at things such as timeframes. Additionally, make sure that you understand exactly what the question is asking of you. It's never a good idea just to throw everything you know at an essay. Think about what's relevant to the question being asked, then cater your knowledge to it.

2. Take planning seriously.

The best essays come about from meticulous research and planning. Some people spend only a little amount of time on the planning stage of their essay, leaving the bulk of the work for the writing stage. While this may work for some people, what you'll likely find is that you've forgotten something when planning and now have to find a place for it in your essay. This can result in a messy structure, and your essay can lose focus.

The best way to avoid this is to devote more time to the planning stage of your essay. Your plan should be as robust as possible, briefly detailing each section and paragraph. This way, you'll probably end up doing most of the work in the planning stage of the essay-writing process.

Once your plan is finished, and you're happy with the flow of it, then you should start writing the essay. You might find that the actual essay-writing part is easy – all you're doing is turning all of the points you've made in your plan into full sentences and paragraphs. This also means that you can spot any problems with your essay in the earliest stage, before you've done the bulk of the actual writing. Finally, a strong essay plan will let you know where your argument is going before you've started writing, meaning you can tighten up your ideas rather than just make things up as you go along.

3. Make your essay laser-focused.

Don't *literally* write an essay on lasers. Instead, make sure that your essay is incredibly focused, since this will stop your work from trying to take on too much. Make sure you answer the question, but don't be afraid to take a narrow focus. It's almost always better to go in-depth on a small number of issues, rather than have a shallow analysis of lots of issues. At degree level, your work needs to have depth, so be willing to sacrifice breadth in order to get it.

For example, if a question requires you to use case studies to support your argument, consider looking at just one in more detail, rather than many in brief. This will also help you from going off on a tangent if you force yourself to narrow your focus.

Finally, having a very narrow focus gives you the opportunity to be original in a way that doesn't make sweeping generalisations. A very specific scope gives you the opportunity to go into detail on a minute area, which in turn might give you the chance to say something truly unique.

4. Be concise.

Flowery language and long words aren't always the most appropriate when writing an essay. Of course, you should have some kind of writing style, but this doesn't mean that you need to become incomprehensible. You should aim to make your language easy to understand, with sentence structure that doesn't spiral out of control. As a general rule, short sentences are preferable to longer ones, since you can prevent run-on sentences and a general lack of focus. The goal of an essay is to convey an argument, not to show off with fancy sentence structure. Be sensible and cut out nonsense.

5. Avoid clichés.

One of the most important things to remember when trying to get a first in your next essay is to avoid clichés. This is vital because whoever is marking your work doesn't want to be bored by the same ideas, phrases, and rhetorical devices. For instance, grand-standing is a cliché which detracts from the focus of an essay, and makes it more generic.

Here's an example of grand-standing:

"Since the <u>dawn of human civilisation</u>, scholars have discussed what it means to be human..."

While this might be the case, it's very unlikely that opening your essay with this phrase will be of any use to your argument. It doesn't shine any light on what you're going to say – all it does is waste space, which could be spent on meaningful discussion. Clichés like this don't come across as confident – it looks clumsy. As we mentioned previously, try and keep your argument to the point, rather than relying on rhetorical devices.

6. Paraphrasing is better than writing quotations.

Throughout your education, you might have been taught to quote from sources very frequently. While it's vital that you back up any claim that you make with evidence, a quote often isn't the best way to do so. Let's take a look at why.

When you use a quote as evidence, you'll probably be using it in the following format:

1. Introduce the point you want to make.

2. Give a quote to support the point.

3. Explain what the quote is saying.

7. Explain how this is relevant to your point, as well as the essay question.

When you explain what the quote is saying, you'll probably end up repeating some of the things that have been said. Therefore, you've wasted some space by writing the quote, then putting it in your own words. Instead, you can save space (and look more sophisticated) by ditching quotes and just paraphrasing instead. Not only does this save space, but it also proves that you understand the quote and know what you're talking about.

In some cases, however, it might still be relevant to include the full quote. For example, if you're quoting a line from a Shakespeare play, then the structure of the line, as well as the exact wording, is relevant. So, in these cases, you should opt to provide a quote in its entirety.

8. Make sure your referencing is correct and presentable.

When writing an academic essay, good referencing discipline is vital. Find out what system the relevant assessing body prefers (e.g. Harvard referencing, APA, MLA, Chicago/Turabian) and then stick to it strictly. There are plenty of referencing guides online which will show you how to reference every kind of media possible – from written journals to YouTube videos. Go through your entire essay, and make sure that you've cited all of the sources you've used properly. This is an easy way to stop yourself from dropping marks.

9. Be original.

Originality is a tricky area when it comes to writing an essay. The likelihood is that you're not going to be able to change the world in a single essay. Scholars devote their whole lives and thousands of pages to even the smallest of advances in their own fields. You've probably only got a few weeks and maybe a few thousand words.

Likewise, it probably seems as if all the big ideas have already been made. If you find yourself coming up with a radically new idea when writing an essay, the chances are that someone has already written about it. Being original can be incredibly difficult.

However, if you make your focus in an essay extremely narrow (as previously mentioned), you have a bit more room to work in. In a few thousand words, you aren't going to come up with a whole new theory. However, you might be able to make a small but meaningful difference within a narrow field. Try to narrow your focus in your next essay, in order to show some original thought.

10. Be confident.

Like originality, it's important to show confidence in your essays. After all, an essay is an argument, and the marker wants to see you get behind your ideas, rather than sit on the fence. You don't want to come across as foolhardy or blind to criticism, but don't be afraid to make strong claims if you have evidence to support them.

If you have space and time, try to address possible criticisms of your own argument. You can either address criticisms as you go, or devote a section towards the end of your essay on all the possible issues one might have with your ideas. Awareness of criticisms (as well as the ability to refute them) will show a level of sophistication that will put you far ahead of the competition.

11. Avoid lengthy introductions and conclusions.

Getting started on an essay is possibly the hardest part. Figuring out what you're going to say in the opening sentence can be a stumbling block, and it might be tempting just to start writing mindlessly. However, try to avoid this – you'll most likely ramble on, rather than getting to the point of your argument. Try to save introductions and conclusions for the very end of the writing stage of your essay. Once you know what you've said in the main body of your argument, you'll know what to write in the introduction and conclusion. This will help you to keep these sections laser-focused.

PROOFREADING

Proofreading is an essential part of the writing process for any kind of educational assessment. Whether you're solving Maths questions, writing an essay, or making a presentation, it's vital that you check for errors. When proofreading, you should look out for the following:

- Spelling, grammar, and punctuation errors;

- Inappropriate vocabulary;

- Unclear points;

- Messy paragraphs and sections;

- Sources without proper referencing;

- Factual errors.

Since this is a lot to keep an eye out for, you should probably do at least two proofreads of your work. On the first proofread, look out for the bigger issues, then move onto smaller errors such as typos in a later proofread, once you're happy with the content.

Another tip for proofreading is to wait for a little while after finishing a draft before reading it. If you start proofreading as soon as you've finished writing, you might be too burnt out to catch the issues. So, once you've finished writing your assignment, leave it for a couple of hours before taking a look at it. This way, you'll be looking at it with a 'fresh' pair of eyes, and you'll be more likely to spot things that need fixing.

Finally, if it's possible, have someone you trust take a look over your work. Even if they aren't an expert in the area you're writing on, they'll be able to tell you if there are spelling, grammar, and punctuation errors. Likewise, they'll probably be able to spot things which are unclear or messy. However, remember to be careful who you show your work to – someone might try to steal your ideas!

Plagiarism

Plagiarism is the act of taking someone else's work and, whether knowingly or unknowingly, try to pass it off as your own. This is an issue that is *extremely* serious, and with good reason. For university students, punishments for plagiarism will vary depend on the severity of the case, but it isn't impossible for them to end in expulsion from the university. For this reason, it's vital that you avoid plagiarism in your work.

As previously mentioned, one of the best ways to avoid plagiarism is to make sure that you correctly cite any information as a source. Think of it this way: if you got the idea from somewhere else, then you need to make that clear in your work. This is why you should make note of everything that you're reading for your assignment – you'll have a record of everything you've learned, and where you got it from.

Of course, it's very unlikely that any idea that you've come up with is completely original. The chances are, at some point, someone else has thought of the same thing, and they might even have published it. In these cases, you should make use of search engines to look up what you've written, and see if there are reputable sources which support it. If this is the case, then you should cite this source in your work as evidence.

Referencing

Referencing is an essential part of most assessed projects at school or university. In particular, students studying for essay-based subjects should train themselves to reference sources properly so that their work looks professional and so they also avoid accusations of plagiarism.

If you are at university, depending on the university, course, and module, the type of referencing system that you'll have to use will differ. Some departments might be more relaxed about which referencing system you use, so long as you make sure that you are consistent. Your department should specify the referencing system that you need to use.

The following are some of the most prominent referencing systems in higher education, as well as (roughly) which subjects they apply to:

Referencing System	Format	Example
APA	Author (last name and initials). (Year of publication). *Title of book*. Place of publication: Publication.	Smith, J. (2013). *How to Reference*. London: How2become Ltd.
Chicago	Last name, First name. *Title of book*. Place of publication: Publisher, Year of publication.	Smith, John. *How to Reference*. London: How2become Ltd, 2013.
Harvard	Name of author(s) (last name and initials). (Year of publication). *Title of book*. Place of publication: Publisher.	Smith, J. (2013). *How to Reference*. London: How2become Ltd.
MLA	Last name, First name. *Title of book*. Publisher, Year of Publication.	Smith, John. *How to Reference*. How2become Ltd, 2013.
Vancouver	Name of authors(s) (last name and initials). *Title of book*. Place of publication: Publisher; Year of publication.	Smith, J. *How to Reference*. London: How2become Ltd; 2013.

Applicable Subjects	Notes
Social Sciences (e.g. Psychology or Sociology)	
History and Economics	
Arts and Humanities	Variant of the APA System
Arts and Humanities	
Medicine and Science	

Bear in mind that the examples above only demonstrate how to reference a book with a single author. Each referencing system has different formats for each type of work that you're referencing. On the next page, we've included some examples:

Edited books	Books with multiple authors	E-Books and pdf documents	Specific chapters of edited books
Newspaper articles	Online newspaper articles	Journals	Online journals
Websites	Blogs	Online publications	YouTube videos
Films	CDs	Lyrics	Religious texts
Acts of Parliament	Press releases	Interviews	Patent documents
Social media	Apps	Podcasts	Maps
Unpublished works	Video games	Archived documents	Annual reports

Each referencing system will have its own rules regarding each of these types of source. Before including one of these sources in your work, find out the exact format. It's also worth remembering that, when including citations in your work, you will need to cite sources as you go and include them in a bibliography.

The first of these is straightforward. Depending on the rules set by your referencing system or university, you will have to either cite sources *in-text* or by using *footnotes*.

Here's an example of an in-text citation in the Harvard referencing style:

Smith (2013, p. 135) notes that some universities prefer in-text citations.

This citation denotes the year that the book was published, as well as the exact page number it is referring to.

The alternative to the in-text method is to create a footnote. This is essentially the same as the in-text method, except the citation information appears at the bottom of the page:

In his book, Smith notes that other universities and referencing systems prefer the use of footnotes.[1]

The footnotes system is sometimes preferable because it can prevent the text from becoming too cluttered. Most word-processing programs are capable of automating the footnoting system, making it easy to do.

____

[1] Smith (2013), p. 136.

Once you've cited all of your sources in text and written your assignment, you'll need to construct a bibliography. This is a summary of all the works that you've used when writing your own assignment.

If you are at university, the contents of your bibliography will differ depending on your subject and department. Some prefer you to include everything that you've read regarding the topic of your assignment, even if you haven't referenced it in your work. Otherwise, they will ask you to only include works that you've referenced. Find out the conventions that your university has set before completing your bibliography.

Bibliographies should be filled out in alphabetical order by the surname of the author. So, 'Johnson, S.' would appear before 'Smith, J.'

A final tip for making referencing as easy as possible is to write a bibliography while you're gathering your research. This way, all you'll need to do is copy and paste the same bibliography into your assignment when you're finished with it. This is also a great method for keeping track of what you've read during the research stage, meaning you won't have to trawl back through your notes and books to find exact page numbers.

GETTING TOP MARKS

Now that we've taken a look at the assignment flowchart and touched on each area, let's look at some expert tips for each major stage of the assignment-writing process.

Planning Your Coursework

In many ways, the planning stage of the assignment-writing process is the most important part of submitting an excellent piece of work. If you create a proper plan, then the bulk of the work you need to do will already be finished when you get to the main writing stage.

Treat the planning stage as though you were writing up the actual piece of work, but in a more condensed format. Try to create every point of your argument, with evidence and explanations, and put it inside your plan.

On top of this, divide these into paragraphs and sections, and make a note of ways in which each of them relate to the question and to the previous section. By doing this, you should create a plan that smoothly goes through every major point of your work. An essay or any other kind of written assignment which flows properly will have a much better chance of scoring high marks than one that feels clunky or disjointed.

As we've recommended in the flowchart above, you should try to create two plans for your coursework. The first is a rough plan that outlines the general direction of your argument, as well as some basic points. Once you've done all of your research, you can adapt this plan to create a more fleshed-out one.

Conducting Research

After planning, research is one of the most important parts of writing an assignment. No matter what course you're taking, if you fail to provide evidence for your argument, then you will get very few marks. Without conducting thorough research, you won't have the evidence you need in order to create a piece of work that matches university standards.

In particular, try to do the following when it comes to gathering information for your coursework:

1. Start by using recommended reading lists provided by the department. This will be a curated list of sources which are relevant to your topic. In addition, they *should* be books, journals, and other types of source which are suited to your level of study.

2. Make use of *reputable* online sources alongside books. By 'reputable', we mean journals and other works that have been formally published/peer reviewed.

3. Unless specified otherwise, try not to use amateur blog posts or online encyclopaedias.

If you find a source that you aren't sure about, get in touch with your lecturer or seminar leader.

When it comes to research, you should have a wide range of resources available.

The first port of call should be your university library. Try to get hold of the most essential books from the recommended reading list as soon as possible, since these are the most likely to be taken out by someone else. Once you've got these, read the relevant chapters and take notes on anything that might be useful to your assignment, as well as the page numbers. Get all of the information you need as soon as possible, just in case the book gets recalled and you have to return it.

If you've exhausted all of the relevant materials in the library, get yourself online and see what you can access there. Quite often, universities will give you login details for online journals and journal search engines, giving you access to a wealth of articles and other material that might be useful for your work. Be sure to reference these correctly, since they must be cited in a slightly different way to print journals.

If you don't have access to any of these, some of the sources you need might be accessible in other places. In particular, extremely old works such as Ancient Greek philosophical texts can often be found in their entirety online and free of charge. Of course, more recent works will not be available in this way for copyright reasons.

If this doesn't cover everything, try and find some students on your course in the years above you. If you're lucky, they might have a copy of the book that you need that they could lend to you. If your university has a mentoring network set up between students across years, then this might be a great opportunity to get hold of key materials.

If there are still resources that you need after taking these steps, then you might have to buy the books yourself. When doing this, make sure you buy the correct edition of the book, since different publications of the same book might not be quite as relevant. This is especially the case for translated works, where there might be a large disparity between two separate translations. Reading lists set by departments and modules should include the exact versions you need if this is the case.

Once you have all of the sources you need, it's time to get reading and note-making. When it comes to coursework, it's often better to write out the key information in exact quotes. This is so that you don't exactly re-word something in a way which changes the meaning of the sentence. While you should almost always paraphrase rather than quote directly when writing your assignment, re-writing the quote in full at this stage is preferable. Remember to keep track of page numbers so that referencing is easier later on.

Although most research that students conduct involves reading and taking notes from articles, some courses might require lab work for assignments. In these cases, the work you will need to complete will be set out for you, and you'll likely be given a slot to do the lab work. Once you've finished it, you'll probably need to write a report on it. The tips in this chapter will apply to writing a lab report, but be sure to consult documents from your department which might specify conventions and formatting styles.

Once you've gathered all of the research you need, we strongly suggest adding the relevant information to your plan, fleshing it out even more. You might find that the plan you wrote before doesn't quite work in light of what you've learned from research. This isn't a problem: re-write your plan until it suits the kind of argument you want to make.

Writing Your Assignment

Once you've finished planning and researching, it's time to write your piece of work. If you've planned well, this shouldn't be too difficult a task; all you're really doing is turning short bullet points into full sentences. However, there are some tips you can take on board to improve your chances of getting the top grades.

Write the Introduction and Conclusion Last

Sometimes, figuring out a great introduction can be difficult. You want to avoid opening with grandiose, sweeping statements, but you also want to give a general idea of what your argument is. If you've planned properly, you should already know the shape and direction of your argument. However, it's usually better to jump straight into the main body of work. Then, you can write a fully focused and sharp introduction.

Once you've finished writing everything, then you can head back and write a great introduction and conclusion based on what's in the main part of your assignment.

Keep Things Simple

You might be aware of the famous adage from *Hamlet* which states that 'brevity is the soul of wit'. In other words, you should not waste the reader's time; explain points properly, but in as few words as necessary.

In addition, you don't always need to use overly complicated terminology. In some cases, you'll have no choice but to, but in many cases simpler language is preferable. In some subjects, you might be marked specifically on the wealth of your vocabulary and your grasp on language. In these cases, you can be more decadent with your terms.

Another way to keep things simple is to use shorter sentences. The longer a sentence is, the more unwieldy it can become. In turn, this might lead to run-on sentences which are more difficult to read than shorter sentences. Experiment with the length of your sentences to see if making them shorter gives your work more clarity. If you have been tasked with writing an essay in which you present a specific argument, you will have to adjust your preparations accordingly. Let's get straight into how you should go about this.

ACHIEVING 'ACADEMIC STYLE'

If you think of an argument as a building or architectural project, then the research stage is the part where you do your initial planning. Here, you're gathering information about the topic you're studying, in the same way an architect might find out about the lay of the land where they're tasked to build. The key message here is that, without research, your essay can't get off the ground.

The first major step to constructing a great argument is to know what you're talking about. On top of this, it helps to know what the arguments of those around you are as well, such as notable scholars. You can draw upon the ideas of others to help strengthen your argument, and use the evidence found by them to support you.

In addition, you need to know what opponents of your viewpoint believe, so that you can refute their ideas properly. After all, you can't make a well-constructed argument if you don't know what you're up against, and aren't aware of the possible criticisms or alternatives levelled at your beliefs.

In this chapter, we'll be taking a look at how to use your own research of a position to help you strengthen your argument. The areas we will be examining are the following:

- How to organise your research;

- Making use of other people's arguments;

- Criticising opposition viewpoints.

HOW TO ORGANISE YOUR RESEARCH

When it comes to organising your research, you should try to place everything useful you find into categories. Here are some examples of areas you should try to cover in your research:

1. **Background information on the issue** – Data, terminology, and other pieces of information that don't necessarily belong to a certain side of a debate. These will form a part of the 'bedrock' for your own argument.

2. **Arguments in favour of your own central thesis** – These are ideas presented by other people that you can refer to in your argument. When including them, make sure that you reference them correctly, so that you aren't accused of plagiarism.

3. **Evidence for your own central thesis** – Supporting evidence will hold up your own arguments, and therefore your central thesis, under scrutiny. Without strong evidence, most arguments will not be taken seriously.

4. **Other central theses in line with your own** – These are central theses which have been devised by other writers and thinkers which, although they don't necessarily say the same thing as you, are compatible with your ideas.

5. **Other central theses which contradict your own** – These are central theses which are

not compatible with your own. In many cases, these will be arguments that you need to refute.

6. **Evidence for opposing central theses –** This is the evidence for the perspectives which contradict your own argument. You might find yourself picking holes in this evidence to destabilise the opposing argument.

7. **Potential criticisms of your own central thesis –** You need to keep on the lookout for existing criticisms of your own arguments. This way, you can pre-emptively address them in your own argument.

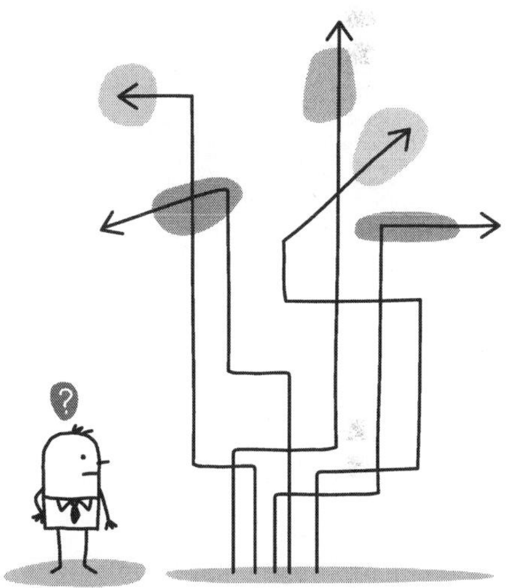

MAKING USE OF OTHER PEOPLE'S ARGUMENTS

When you're arguing for a position, you should probably mention the viewpoints of others which either actively support your central thesis or are simply compatible with it.

For example, let's imagine that you're trying to defend the position that foreign aid should be cut to ensure that there is enough money for people in your own country. You might find that there's another thinker who believes the same thing, which makes their arguments incredibly valuable to yours. You can refer to the arguments made by other people in order to support your own perspective, but make sure that you cite them with a proper referencing system. This is so you can avoid accusations of plagiarism.

In addition, you need to take note of the criticisms of the arguments that you're making use of, and be ready to respond to them if you use other writers' ideas to support your own central thesis.

CRITICISING OPPOSING VIEWPOINTS

When conducting research on your topic, you're bound to come across plenty of arguments opposing the position you've chosen to defend. The question you've been asked to argue might even include one of these criticisms, or specify that you must respond to a counterargument. In these cases, you need to be prepared to respond to them.

When approaching opposing views, your first goal should be to try and demonstrate how their argument doesn't work in the context you're working with. Perhaps you can do this by highlighting faulty reasoning on their part, or by refuting the premises that they rely on. We'll cover how to deal with criticisms and counterarguments in the coming section *Counterarguments and Criticism.*

At the researching stage, keep an eye out for opposing arguments that you might have to face. If it helps, rank the arguments from most difficult to refute, to least difficult. You won't have space to address every criticism of an argument, so pick your battles wisely and choose one which is most relevant to the area you're debating.

Additionally, you should look for criticisms of these counterarguments. It might be the case that another thinker has already delivered a critical blow to these opposing arguments, meaning that you can use their words to support your own response. Keep track of these when researching for your argument, and categorise them so you know which counterarguments correspond to different positions.

Conclusion

Now you should have a good idea about how to research and organise information for your argument. Keep the following in mind when conducting your research:

1. Organise all of your research into categories, such as those we described earlier in this chapter.

2. Feel free to use other people's arguments to support your own perspective, as long as you reference them correctly.

3. Be prepared to respond to criticism by researching possible counterarguments beforehand.

In the next chapter, we'll be taking a look at how to start planning and forming your argument.

PLANNING ACADEMICALLY

Once you've completed your research on the position you're defending, and the possible opponents, you need to start planning your own response. If we continue the architecture analogy from earlier on, this is the equivalent of laying the foundations of your building. Without a good foundation, a building is unsafe and could fall apart.

In theory, you could write or otherwise give an argument without this stage. However, you'd quickly find that the foundations of the building you've made are shaky, and probably quite easy to pick holes in. For this reason, it's best to take the formation stage of an argument seriously. By this, we mean that you need to plan your argument.

HOW TO PLAN YOUR ARGUMENT

Planning the specific academic argument within your essay is very similar to planning the essay itself. By this, we mean that the process for planning one can easily be translated to the other with only a few minor changes.

The following flowchart should give you a strong idea as to how you should plan an academic argument:

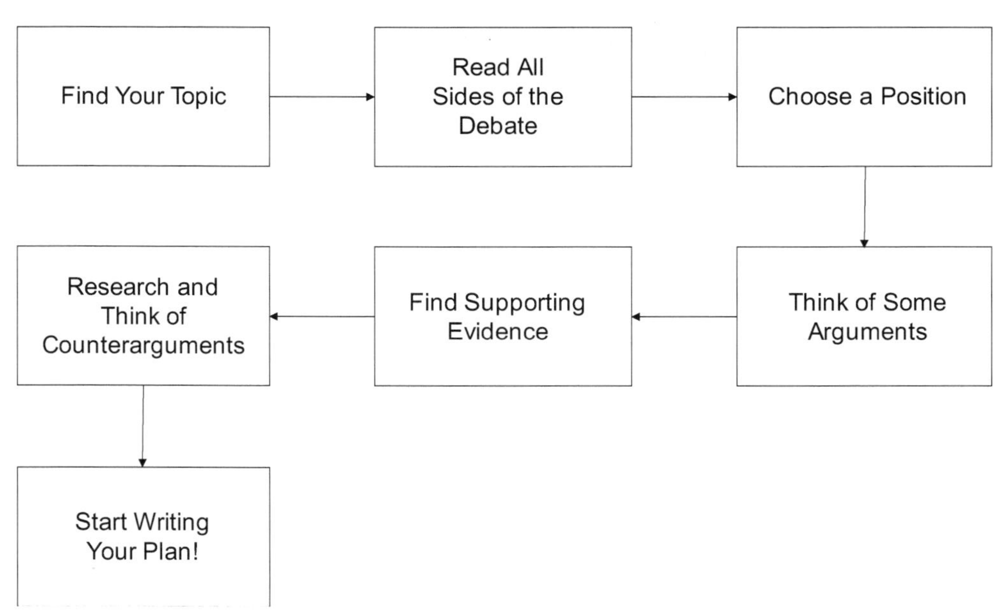

Let's take a look at each of these steps in more detail.

Find Your Topic

The first step in writing an argument is to know what you're actually going to be arguing over. Find out the following:

- What the topic is;

- What the main sides of the argument are;

- Why the topic is important;

- Some context to how the topic fits in with the bigger picture (e.g. how religious moral systems play into the larger subject of ethics).

Read All Sides of the Debate

Once you have a rough idea about the topic you're going to be writing about or speaking on, you need to know all sides of the debate. Even though you're ultimately going to pick one side, you need to 'know your enemy' in the sense that you need to understand their perspective. Take this time to read up on all sides of the debate thoroughly.

Note: Often, there's more than two sides to any single debate. Try to find nuance in the major positions to see if there are alternatives that you could investigate.

Choose a Position

Depending on what your argument is being used for, you might not be able to choose your position. For example, you might be allocated a position on a specific topic, or be forced to take a specific side.

However, if you have the opportunity to choose your position, spend some time considering which argument you think you have more to say about. It also helps if you're passionate about that side of the debate, but that isn't vital. Choose the position which you think will allow you to say something interesting.

Whatever the case, **you must end up taking a clear stance**. Examiners won't look kindly on someone who has tried to sit on the fence between two or more positions.

Come up with Some Arguments

Once you've chosen your position, it's time to think of the main argument for it, or the main argument against the position that you're attacking. You should try to think of one major line of argument, which should be made up of lots of small arguments or points. This main line of argument will be your **central thesis**: the main thing that you're trying to say. We'll discuss argumentative structure in more detail later in this chapter, but for now remember that each point of your argument should contribute to the overall conclusion.

Find Supporting Evidence

Once you have some ideas, it's time to find evidence to either support them or disprove them. Go through each of your potential arguments and look for supporting evidence as well as counterarguments. If you think an argument is untenable due to too many flaws, then ditch it and focus on the rest. Over time, you should end up with only the strongest arguments remaining.

Research and Think of Counterarguments

If you followed the previous point, you should already have some potential counterarguments for your strongest points. If not, you need to come up with some yourself. Thinking of counterarguments is important for the following reasons:

1. If you think of the counterargument yourself, you have the time to address it properly. Sometimes, this might mean you can think of a strong response, but in other cases you may just have to concede.

2. Acknowledging counterarguments, whether you're able to defeat them or not, shows a level of sophistication and holistic reasoning in your argument.

3. If you're in a debate, knowing the possible criticisms of your position means that you'll

be ready to respond effectively, making you more confident in your argument.

Once you have all of the above areas researched and covered, you need to start thinking about how all of your ideas are going to fit together. This will be the focus of the next few sections.

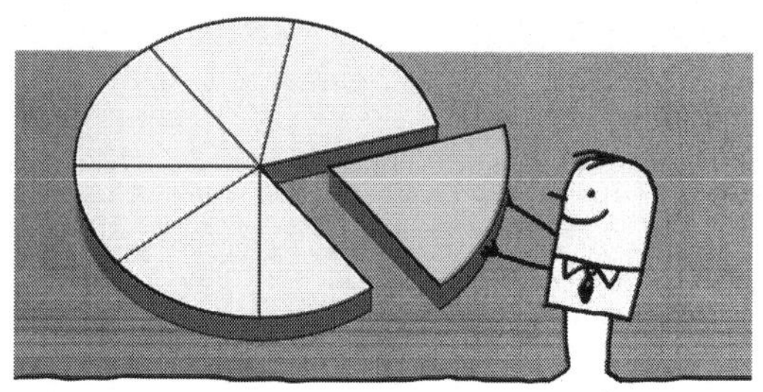

ARGUMENT STRUCTURE

When it comes to forming an argument, it isn't enough to have great content. You could have the strongest claims and best evidence in the world, but if your argument isn't structured correctly, people will struggle to follow it, find it clunky or unintuitive, and perhaps just be bored by it. Part of the point of an argument is to convince others that your position is correct, and the best way to do this is to form a well-structured viewpoint, that comes across as confident.

Good argument structure is also helpful for yourself. A smooth 'flow' to your line of argument will make it stick in your mind more easily, making the writing stage of the argument simpler. Whatever the case, you should spend as much time as possible considering how your argument is structured.

Argument Structure – Single Paragraph

When writing an essay, your work should of course take the form of multiple paragraphs or sections. These will act as small 'chunks' of argument that work together to come to your conclusion. So, the structure of each single paragraph or section is vital, as each piece adds up to the total. Let's take a look at some ways that you can structure a single paragraph or section properly.

Firstly, a good general rule to follow is that each paragraph should be devoted to a single point. In other words, you shouldn't try and tackle more than one main point in a single paragraph, although it might be necessary to cover one point over multiple paragraphs. This is because, essentially, the structure of a paragraph should mirror the overall structure of an essay.

An essay has an introduction, main body, and conclusion. In most cases, single paragraphs and sections benefit from the same structure and principles. Each paragraph should begin with a sentence introducing the main point, followed by the meat of the point you're trying to make. Finally, a 'conclusion' to the paragraph links the content in the paragraph to the overall point of the argument.

You might be familiar with the 'PEEL' technique – a more than adequate way to structure arguments, especially if you feel less confident in doing so. Let's break the parts of the 'PEEL' technique down:

Point – This is the main point that you want to make in a single paragraph.

Evidence – Once you've outlined your main point, give the evidence that justifies it.

Explain – Explain what this evidence means for your main point.

Link – Link the entirety of your point to the line of argument so far.

With the above advice on adding an introduction and conclusion to every paragraph, the technique looks like this:

Introduction – Introduce the main point of the paragraph, in brief.

Point – This is the main point that you want to make in a single paragraph.

Evidence – Once you've outlined your main point, give the evidence that justifies it.

Explain – Explain what this evidence means for your main point.

Link – Link the entirety of your point to the line of argument so far.

Conclusion – Bring the point of this paragraph to a close whilst leading into the next.

Admittedly, 'IPEELC' doesn't have quite the same memorable quality as 'PEEL', but nevertheless gives you a good idea about how to structure an argument.

Once you have an idea about how you're going to structure a paragraph, you should consider how long it's going to be. There's no easy guideline on how long a paragraph should be, but instead try and make sure that your paragraphs are all of approximately the same length. If you have lots of small paragraphs, followed by a gigantic one, then this might suggest that your argument isn't balanced properly. It's a good idea to avoid huge paragraphs since the reader or audience can end up getting 'bogged down' in it. This can kill the pace of your argument.

If you commit to making sure only one major point is covered in each paragraph, this should result in them all being approximately the same length. This will also help your argument appear more evenly paced.

Another key aspect of your argument is how major points are connected to one another. Quite often, arguments will be 'cumulative': the argument will build from early main points, constantly adding new facets and greater nuance as it goes along.

At the very least, you should try to have each major point flow into the next, by using paragraph connectives in the conclusion for the next paragraph. If – for whatever reason – you're about to jump from one main point to another which is somewhat unrelated, make this clear in the argument or essay so the reader knows where they're headed. This is often referred to as **signposting** as it points the reader or audience in the direction that the argument is taking them. This allows them to keep up with your argument, which in turn means that the message of your argument is more likely to reach them as intended.

Argument Structure – Full Argument

Once you've nailed the structure for a single paragraph, it's time to figure out how they're all going to slot together. Here, we're going to take a closer look at the structure of your entire argument.

The way your ideas fit together is vital for how they're communicated. As we mentioned previously, it doesn't matter if your ideas are the best in the world if they aren't communicated effectively. Structuring an argument in a way which will make all of your different ideas work together is the only way to avoid this pitfall.

It may help to think of your argument as a machine of some kind. Each paragraph of an argument, like each part of a machine, fulfils a different function. On its own, each part is adequate in completing its assigned task. However, it's only when these parts all come together that they fulfil their purpose. In the same way, each paragraph or section of your argument should read and make some sense on their own, but will also contribute to the overall essay: the sum of every part of your argument.

It simply isn't enough for each part of the machine, or argument, to be fulfilling their role. They all need to be connected to one another, or to some central place, in order to be able to work together. So, your aim as a writer is to make sure that each point of your argument fits with other points, and contributes to the overall product: your central thesis.

The most straightforward way to ensure that your argument fits together properly is to check every part of the argument in the planning stage. Divide your argument into each point, assigning them either a title which summarises them or even just a letter or number. This way, you can easily keep track of which parts of the argument are interconnected with the others.

At the very least, you need to make sure that every part of your argument contributes to your central thesis. If you have points 1, 2, 3, and 4, but only points 1, 2, and 3 leave an impact on your central thesis, then point 4 isn't a necessary part of your argument. If that's the case, why is it still there?

If you discover that a part of your argument doesn't affect the outcome of it, then you should either:

a)   Think of ways it can be reformulated so that it *is* useful.

b)   Remove it and use that space for something that is substantial.

Once you have every part of your argument connected to the central thesis, you might want to think about how they connect to one another. Generally speaking, it's a good idea for each part of your argument to logically follow on from the previous one, and neatly lead into the next. So, if point 3 requires ideas discussed in point 2 in order to function, then point 3 needs to come over point 2. In many cases, arguments are **cumulative**: ideas discussed earlier on are necessary for later parts to make sense. Make sure that your argument takes a natural form in which each point builds to the central thesis, rather than them darting between different concepts. If you do need to move into a completely new section, state this clearly before moving into it. This gives the reader or audience an idea of where you're headed next.

CONCLUSION

At this point, you should have a good idea about how to form and structure your argument. Try to keep the following in mind:

1. Make sure to read all sides of a debate before choosing your position. This way, you'll be ready to deal with counterarguments.

2. Follow the 'IPEELC' structure for single paragraphs.

3. Make sure that each of your main points contributes to your central thesis, and try to make your points flow into one another neatly.

Now that you've formed your argument, it's time to learn how to write it in a presentable and convincing format!

IMPLEMENTING THE PLAN

By this stage in the process of creating your argument, you've probably done most of the hard work. So far, you've researched the position you're arguing for (as well as the positions you're arguing against), and planned the structure of your argument.

If you've planned well, you've probably even got most of the content ready to go – all that's left is to formulate it in a way which is suitable for submission. In this chapter, we'll discuss how to write your argument in a way which is academically-minded.

The main areas which we'll cover are:

- Argumentative writing conventions;

- Establishing tone;

- Following your plan.

Once you've learned these, you should be in a great position to write an essay containing your argument.

ARGUMENTATIVE WRITING CONVENTIONS

When writing an essay, think about your audience. In reality, the only person who will read your essay is the person or people marking it. This means that, unless you're advised otherwise, you don't have to act as though your reader is completely uninformed on the issue. The person marking your work will be least competent in the area that you've written about, and is most likely an expert. Therefore, you won't need to explain every single tiny facet of your argument – a fair amount will be assumed knowledge.

When considering the audience of your work, you also need to remember to be as formal as possible. This means that colloquialisms (or slang terms) must be avoided entirely unless there's sufficient context for it, such as a quote. Otherwise, stay formal with your language.

On the topic of language, your vocabulary doesn't always have to be flashy or decadent. Usually, you're better off describing your ideas in simpler terms, so that your work is easier to read and understand. Make use of terminology where relevant,

but keeping things simple is a good rule when writing an argument. After all, the most important part of your work is your line of reasoning, not the fancy words you use to embellish it.

Note: in some cases, you'll be marked on your ability to use fancy vocabulary because it will demonstrate your grasp on language. In this instance, feel free to get elaborate with your language, provided that you know what the words you're using actually mean.

THE 'I' PRONOUN

The 'I' pronoun is tricky to use correctly in a written essay, to the point where many will advise against you using it. The issue is that use of 'I' can lead to lazy statements such as 'I think that…' or 'I believe…' These statements aren't useful, because you're often not supporting what you think or believe. This is why you might have been taught in the past to avoid using 'I' pronouns.

However, some cases permit use of the 'I' pronoun as long as you can keep it in check. If you aren't sure whether your course approves of its use, ask a lecturer or supervisor for the subject that you're studying. They will advise you on whether it's appropriate for use.

As a general rule, try to avoid 'I' pronouns if you aren't sure how to use them.

Establishing Tone

When writing an argumentative essay, you need to make sure that the reader is on the same wavelength as you. For this reason, you should try to make your language set a tone which matches the subject matter of your argument.

By 'tone', we essentially mean the mood of your work. Some pieces of writing have a more informal tone, whilst others will opt for formality. Generally speaking, the more formal tone is preferable for any kind of academic essay, since a more comedic or relaxed angle might detract from the important points that you wish to make. For this reason, it's best to leave the jokes and slang terms out of your work.

At the same time, you don't want to be too grave in your argument. Too dark a tone will create a crushing, distracting atmosphere, so try to lighten the mood with less focus on grim details. Of course, you'll sometimes need to discuss dismal ideas, but try to keep these as formal and 'tonally neutral' as possible.

With all of this in mind, you still need to be able to show some artistic flair in your work. You don't need to go overboard, but your own personal touch will make your writing stand out when an examiner is marking it.

FOLLOW YOUR PLAN

Finally, the most important step in writing your argument is to follow your plan. If you've spent enough time and thought on it, your plan should be an excellent guiding force for your argument. In many ways, all you're doing in the writing stage is turning bullet-points and notes into full sentences, as all of your research should already be compiled.

While writing, you might find that your plan hasn't covered something, or you might have a brand-new idea. If this happens, don't worry – go back to your plan and look for a way to insert these additions into your work.

CONCLUSION

You're now well on your way to being able to construct a stellar argument for your next essay. Keep the following in mind when writing your arguments:

1. Try and keep the tone as formal as possible, avoiding slang.

2. You don't have to go overboard with flashy vocabulary. Sometimes, it's best to keep things simple.

3. Stick to your plan to make sure that you don't run off on tangents.

In the next chapter, we'll take a look at counterarguments, criticism, and how to correctly implement them in your work.

COUNTERARGUMENTS AND CRITICISM

When researching, planning, and writing your argument, you're going to come up against criticisms, counterarguments, and objections to the position you're trying to defend. If you want to be taken seriously at an academic level, you need to be prepared to address these responses to your argument.

Responding to counterarguments is, in itself, an art form. In this chapter, we'll take a look at how to deal with counterarguments and criticism by examining the following areas:

1. When to discuss counterarguments in your argument.

2. How to present counterarguments in your own work.

3. How to refute counterarguments in your own work.

WHEN SHOULD I DISCUSS COUNTERARGUMENTS?

Once you reach the planning stage of your argument, you have a choice of how to approach counterarguments. Some people choose to respond to counterarguments immediately where they are relevant. Take a look at the following structure:

Introduction

Argument 1

Counterargument to Argument 1

Response to Counterargument (for Argument 1)

Argument 2

Counterargument to Argument 2

Response to Counterargument (for Argument 2)

The benefit of this approach is that you can raise counterarguments as you go, and so the content in question will still be fresh in the reader's mind. You can do this throughout your argument, allowing your responses to the counterarguments to build cumulatively to your central thesis.

Alternatively, you can save all of the counterarguments until the end of your essay. Here's the structure for it:

Introduction

Argument 1

Argument 2

Argument 3

Argument 4

Counterargument to Argument 1

Response to Counterargument (for Argument 1)

Counterargument to Argument 2

Response to Counterargument (for Argument 2)

Counterargument to Argument 3

Response to Counterargument (for Argument 3)

Counterargument to Argument 4

Response to Counterargument (for Argument 4)

Conclusion

Sometimes, approaching each counterargument as you go can get overly convoluted. The above structure allows you to make things more clear-cut, as long as you specify which argument the counterargument is addressing.

Depending on what you're studying, one approach might be preferable to another. If you aren't sure which is more relevant, ask a member of school or university staff which would be more acceptable.

HOW TO PRESENT A COUNTERARGUMENT

Once you've decided on where you're going to address counterarguments, you need to consider how to frame them properly. If your writing isn't clear, some readers might get confused about whether you support or wish to refute a counterargument that you're presenting. To avoid this, you should introduce a counterargument in the same way that you would approach one of your own points:

1. Provide a short introductory sentence which presents the counterargument.

2. Explain what the counterargument is.

3. Demonstrate how it is relevant to, or how it may damage, the argument you're presenting.

This level of signposting will clearly highlight that this is a counterargument that you want to address, which we will cover in the next section. First, let's consider some other ways in which you can make your presentation of counterarguments even more sophisticated.

Mention the Person (or People) Who Coined It

In an academic argument, the counterarguments you raise should be attributed to a relevant scholar. By attaching their name to their work, you're doing three things:

1. Avoiding plagiarism by not trying to pass off other people's ideas as your own.

2. Demonstrating that you are aware of the wider debate and that you've read work from other writers, not just the primary individuals in question.

3. Giving your reader or audience a place to look for more information if they find your own argument interesting.

So, referring to the individual responsible for the counterargument that you're addressing is incredibly worthwhile. Make sure to cite them properly, using whichever referencing system your school or university specifies.

PRESENT THE COUNTERARGUMENT HONESTLY

When presenting a potentially troublesome counterargument, you may be tempted to present it in a format which is easy for you to tackle. While this might seem like a smart idea, the reality is that you're playing into a trap that any marker or astute opponent will spot immediately. In these cases, you'd be 'putting up a straw man'.

> *To 'put up a straw man' is to misrepresent your opponent's argument, whether intentionally or not. This can involve oversimplification in order to make the opponent's argument easier to attack, or make the argument look more extreme than it actually is.*

Essentially, if you misrepresent someone else's argument, you can't combat it effectively. So, when it comes to criticising your overall argument, you'll be accused of 'dodging' the real problems being highlighted by counterarguments. For this reason, take extra steps to present counterarguments as accurately as possible.

HOW TO REFUTE A COUNTERARGUMENT

Now that you know where and how to present a counterargument, you need to be able to refute it. After all, there's no point including a criticism of your argument to your essay if you have no way of defending yourself!

Refuting a counterargument can be incredibly difficult, especially if you're new to the subject that you're writing about. When you're focusing on your own argument, it can be hard to find the time to research why a certain counterargument is ineffective. This is why we suggest taking potential counterarguments seriously when researching and planning your own argument.

Let's take a look at some tips for how to refute counterarguments in your own essay.

Pick Your Battles

When writing an argument, there are two things you need to bear in mind regarding counterarguments:

1.   You can't beat them all.

2.   Even if you could, you probably don't have time to.

For these reasons, you need to choose the counterarguments you want to address or refute. Ideally, this should be done in the planning stage of your essay or argument, so that you know which counterarguments and criticisms are relevant. Once you have an idea about what you're up against, you can then decide which counterarguments you would like to address.

Make sure you don't pick the most fatal counterarguments unless you have the evidence to support yourself, since you'll waste time planning for an argument that you can't win. Likewise, don't set up easy counterarguments to knock down – you won't impress anyone this way. Find counterarguments that you have the evidence to defeat, but that will also require effort to properly contest.

As a rule, you shouldn't refute a criticism that you haven't properly explained. If you want to contest a counterargument, spend at least one paragraph laying the groundwork for your response by introducing and explaining it sufficiently. Conversely, you should try to avoid introducing a counterargument without refuting it.

You should acknowledge potential counterarguments even if you aren't going to combat them, but give proper reason for it, such as a lack of space or time. This way, the reader won't be surprised by counterarguments appearing out of nowhere. Equally, this means that they won't be left disappointed, because they thought you were going to address a counterargument, only for you to never return to it.

Use Evidence

When it comes to refuting a counterargument, you need to have evidence on hand to prove it wrong. The type of evidence will depend on the area that you're studying. For example, if you're writing a scientific paper, then you'll need to draw upon peer-reviewed data to demonstrate how a counterargument is incorrect. If you're in the area of Philosophy, your evidence is going to be a lot more abstract – focusing on thought experiments, logical inconsistencies, and fallacies. Choose a form of evidence which is suitable for your area of study.

If you've planned effectively, you should already possess the evidence that you need in order to refute a counterargument. You don't need to completely bury the criticism in evidence – just present the strongest piece of data which puts the counterargument into question. Here's an idea of how you might structure your response to a counterargument using evidence:

1. Summary of why the counterargument is false.

2. Deeper explanation of why the counterargument is false, including evidence.

3. Explanation as to how this affects your initial argument (if at all).

Always keep in mind that, without evidence, responses to counterarguments are empty.

CONCLUSION

Now you should have a clear idea about how to deal with counterarguments in written essays. When addressing counterarguments and criticism, try to keep the following in mind:

1. You can address counterarguments either immediately after raising your own argument, or wait until the end of your essay to address each criticism.

2. Present your counterarguments with a similar structure to a usual argument, using the 'IPEELC' method.

3. Present counterarguments as accurately as possible, and avoid putting up a straw man.

4. Don't try to take on every possible counterargument – choose the most relevant ones and focus on them.

5. Make use of evidence that fits your area of study, in order to contest a counterargument.

DIFFERENT ESSAY TYPES

Of course, while a helpful place to start, there is not a one-size-fits-all plan for starting an essay. Throughout your academic career, you will probably be asked to complete several different types of essay. That is to say, the assignments you will receive across varying topics and subjects will ask you to do very different things with your writing.

The two main essay types you will face during your academic career are as follows:

- Compare and contrast;

- Evaluate.

Compare and Contrast

Compare and contrast essays involve evaluating the strengths and weaknesses of opposing concepts relative to each other. While you should discuss the merits and shortcomings of these ideas by themselves or in a wider context, the focus of the essay should be on how the concepts relate to each other.

So, your planning should reflect this. Create a list of similarities and differences between the two ideas in question. This can become the foundation of your plan, and by extension your response.

Evaluate

Briefs of 'evaluate' essays may include the following prompts: 'To what extent...' or 'How far do you agree?'

With these projects, you will have to argue for or against a point of view or school of thought by providing evidence. Alongside this, you will also be called upon to evaluate the provenance and therefore the reliability of your sources.

Again, correctly identifying what the question is asking of you and delivering it is the most important first step. Other than that, use previous sections of this guide to help you plan and form your argument.

INTRODUCTIONS AND CONCLUSIONS

You may have noticed that we've waited until the penultimate chapter to discuss two of the most important parts of any argument: the introduction and conclusion. This is because we believe that introductions and conclusions are best saved for the end when constructing your argument. In this chapter, we'll explain why this is the best course of action, as well as how to put together the best introductions and conclusions to make your arguments even stronger.

WHAT'S THE POINT OF INTRODUCTIONS AND CONCLUSIONS?

While the most important part of any argument is the substance in its main body, you need the right 'frame' for your masterwork to go in. Introductions and conclusions serve this function, as they provide the set-up and summary of your argument respectively.

Jumping straight into the main body of your work is a great way to get started with an argument, but that doesn't mean you should neglect introductions and conclusions. Without the correct framing by the introduction and conclusion, your argument might lack focus or context. Therefore, it's vital that you take the time to learn how to use them effectively.

As the name suggests, the purpose of an introduction is to 'introduce' your argument to the reader, audience, or your opponent. It needs to provide some context of the ensuing argument: why the argument is important, and other questions which might influence or be influenced by your own. If your argument is specifically a response to another made by someone else, then it might also be appropriate to give a summary of it in the introduction. We'll take a closer look at writing the perfect introduction later in this chapter.

As for conclusions, the overall aim is to bring your argument to a close. The conclusion is usually a summary of what you've already said or written, tying your argument in a nice bow so that it flows well. We'll discuss conclusions further later in this chapter, but one thing to bear in mind is that you should *never* introduce whole new ideas in your conclusion. If you think there's something relevant that you missed, go back and find space in the main body of your argument and add it in.

WHY SHOULD I WRITE THEM LAST?

It might seem a bit peculiar to form your introduction at the very end of your argument, but we have good justification for this. Since the introduction and conclusion of your arguments introduce and summarise the main body of your work, you need to have a precise idea about what your argument actually contains before you can give a satisfactory primer or recap of it. By all means, get a rough idea of what you'll say in your introduction and conclusion before writing them, but having a completed body of work finished first will make it much easier to refine them.

The other reason why it's a good idea to write your introduction and conclusion last is because it means you can jump straight into developing your ideas. Coming up with a killer introduction leaves a lot of writers stumped, so skip it for now and head straight for the main argument. Then, once you have your whole argument laid out, you can head back to the beginning and entice the reader with a great introduction.

Now that you know why it's a good idea to leave the introduction and conclusion until the end of the argument-writing process, let's look at how to tackle them.

ONTO THE SCENE – CONSTRUCTING A STELLAR INTRODUCTION

When writing an introduction, we find that the following three aspects should be kept in mind:

1. **Clarity** – Your introduction needs to clearly set out the area of debate that you're covering. Briefly explain what makes your position so important, as well as what your argument actually is.

2. **Accuracy** – Make sure that your introduction is razor-sharp. By this, we mean that you should focus only on what's necessary for your argument. This way, the reader or audience has a strong idea of the direction that your argument will take. Try and lay out the main points of your argument in brief during your introduction.

3. **Brevity** – Don't waste the reader or audience's time, and don't waste your own space. The introduction needs to be fairly brief – quickly outlining everything we've spoken about in the above two points.

As you can see, introductions are at their best when they're to-the-point and cut out nonsense. Try and cut straight to the chase. If you're writing an essay, you might want to open like this:

*"The aim of this argument is to demonstrate how advances in our understanding about human origins weren't **revolutionary**, but in fact **evolutionary.**"*

Here, the goal of this argument is neatly summed up by a sentence which gets to the point, is accurate in its terms, and doesn't grand-stand unnecessarily. It also has the added benefit of sparking the audience's imagination, setting them up for the rest of the introduction which will go into slightly more detail.

Once you've nailed your opening sentence, it's time to look a bit closer at what you're arguing about. If you're new to writing arguments, you might want to keep things simpler, rather than get flashy with fancy techniques. **Remember our three rules: clarity, accuracy, and brevity.** Then, apply them to the following steps.

1. Clearly show what it is you're arguing for, and what approach you're going to take. This should be a single, continuous line of argument. If you want, you can lay out each step of your argument here. This will give sufficient signposting to the reader or audience

so that they can follow your argument more easily.

2. Briefly make note of possible criticisms of your argument, and either specify whether you will approach these as you go, or tackle all of them towards the end of your argument.

3. Tell them how all of the things you've mentioned will result in your conclusion. Here, you should say something to the tune of "points *A*, *B*, and *C*, combined with the response to counterargument *X*, will result in conclusion *Z*."

4. If you want, you can end your introduction with a sentence to lead into your first point. However, this isn't always necessary since you can introduce your first point at the start of the next paragraph.

On top of this, make sure that you don't discuss any ideas that won't be referred to throughout your argument. These kinds of red herrings can set false expectations for the reader or audience, and can ultimately make your argument more confusing. This is why we suggest writing your introduction after you've finished writing the main body of work – once you have all of it written, you'll know which ideas to include in your introduction.

The length of your introduction will vary depending on how long your body of work is. For shorter essays and arguments, your introduction shouldn't be any longer than the paragraphs in the main body of your argument. Additionally, your introduction should only be a paragraph long. As a general rule, if your introduction is so long that it needs to be split into more than one paragraph, then it's probably *too* long. There may of course be a few exceptions where it is appropriate to divide your introduction into two paragraphs, but these are the exception rather than the rule.

EXIT STAGE LEFT – WRITING THE PERFECT CONCLUSION

The only way to round off a great body of work is with a conclusion. Conclusions are vital for the following reasons:

1. They remind your reader or audience of everything you've covered in your argument, so that they can visualise the path that your piece has taken.

2. You can re-contextualise every point that you've made, bringing them all together for the end.

The best conclusions are ones which bring the reader back to the beginning, giving them a moment to recap on everything that they've read, whilst reiterating the driving point of your argument. If you've written your argument well, the reader or audience shouldn't have had a significant issue following everything you've said, but rounding it off in a conclusion is a good idea anyway. Even if the recap isn't entirely necessary because your argument was easy to follow, it gives the argument some closure.

When it comes to writing your conclusion, make use of the same three points we discussed in the previous section on introductions: **clarity, accuracy, and brevity**. While your conclusion serves a very different function to the introduction, they should both be approached in a similar fashion.

1. **Clarity** – In clear language, remind the reader of what you've already covered, and how all of this connects to your main point of argument.

2. **Accuracy** – Using the terms that you've defined, bring your argument to a close.

3. **Brevity** – Don't waffle on for long about irrelevant details. Summarise your argument in as few words as possible.

On top of these three guidelines, here are a few more tips for crafting the perfect conclusion.

Don't Introduce New Ideas

As mentioned before, one of the worst things you can do when writing a conclusion is to bring in a new idea. If your argument contained ideas *A*, *B*, *C*, and *D*, you should only refer to these ideas **only** in your conclusion. If you haven't discussed an idea already in your argument, **do not** introduce it in your conclusion.

If it's really such an important concept that you might have missed, go back and try and find a place for it. Otherwise, leave it out. Introducing new ideas in the conclusion has the effect of making your argument look rushed or poorly considered.

Don't Get Grandiose

Just like how grand-standing can weaken your introduction, grandiose statements in your conclusion waste space and time, whilst offer nothing to your argument. It's fine to have a bit of flair, and perhaps hint at the greater implications of your argument, but don't act as though your argument is the most profound thing in the world. Some humility will go a long way, and make your argument seem more sophisticated, as opposed to melodramatic.

CONCLUSION

Now you should have a good idea about how to construct great introductions and conclusions to act as bookends for arguments. When writing your introductions and conclusions, keep the following in mind:

1. Write your introduction and conclusion *after* the rest of your work. This way, you'll know exactly what to include in both of them.

2. Avoid grand-standing in your introductions and conclusions. Stick to the point and get rid of any unnecessary waffle.

3. Keep your introductions and conclusions as short as possible whilst also including all of the core, necessary components.

4. Don't introduce any new ideas in your conclusion. If it's important enough that it needs mentioning, find a place for it in the main body of your argument.

CONCLUSION

You've now reached the end of *Rapid Skills for Students: Successful Essay Planning*. By using this book, you've given yourself the skills necessary to research, plan, and write arguments that are sophisticated and robust – a huge bonus for students looking to up their game academically. If you're heading into academic essays or exams, bear the information in this book in mind whilst revising and planning your work.

A FEW FINAL WORDS...

For any test, it is helpful to keep the following in mind...

The Three 'P's

1. Preparation. Preparation is key to passing any test; you won't be doing yourself any favours by not taking the time to prepare. Many fail their tests because they did not know what to expect or did not know what their own weaknesses were. Take the time to go over any areas you may have struggled with. By doing this, you will become familiar with how you will perform on the day of the test.

2. Perseverance. If you set your sights on a goal and stick to it, you are more likely to succeed. Obstacles and setbacks are common when trying to achieve something great, and you shouldn't shy away from them. Instead, face the tougher parts of the test, even if you feel defeated. If you need to, take a break from your work to relax and then return with renewed vigour. If you fail the test, take the time to consider why you failed, gather your strength and try again.

3. Performance. How well you perform will be the result of your preparation and perseverance. Remember to relax when taking the test and try not to panic. Believe in your own abilities, practise as much as you can, and motivate yourself constantly. Nothing is gained without hard work and determination, and this applies to how you perform on the day of the test.

WANT TO LEARN EVEN MORE REVISION TRICKS?

CHECK OUT OUR OTHER REVISION GUIDES:

Achieve 100% Series

FOR MORE INFORMATION ON OUR REVISION GUIDES, PLEASE CHECK OUT THE FOLLOWING:

WWW.HOW2BECOME.COM

Rapid Study Skills for Students Series

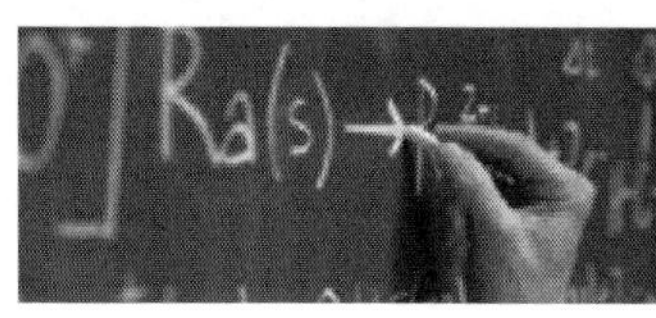

Get Access To

FREE Psychometric

Tests

www.PsychometricTestsOnline.co.uk

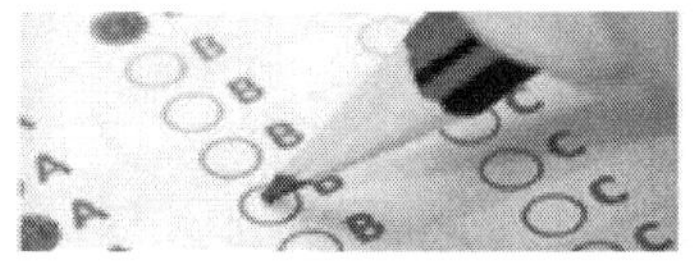

Printed and bound by CPI Group (UK) Ltd, Croydon, CR0 4YY

06/07/2026

02157570-0006